The family CHALLENGE

Passing the Faith from Your Heart to Theirs

By Dr. Scott Turansky
and Joanne Miller, RN, BSN

Dear Reader,

This book contains five selected chapters from a larger book entitled ***Disciplemaking at Home: Raising Kids to Follow After God***, by Dr. Scott Turansky and Joanne Miller, RN, BSN. The five chapters chosen for this book stand alone and communicate a powerful message to parents about passing the faith on to their kids. You don't have to have the larger book to gain the benefit from this smaller one. If you want the complete book, you can go to biblicalparenting.org to learn more.

May God touch your heart and empower you to pass the faith from your heart to the hearts of your children.

Blessings,

Scott Turansky and Joanne Miller

National Center for Biblical Parenting
76 Hopatcong Drive, Lawrenceville, NJ 08648-4136

THE FAMILY CHALLENGE
PASSING THE FAITH FROM YOUR HEART TO THEIRS
©2012 by National Center for Biblical Parenting.

First eBook release, 2012
First Printing, August 2012

Library of Congress Cataloging-in-Publication Data

The Family Challenge
Passing the Faith from Your Heart to Theirs
Dr. Scott Turansky and Joanne Miller, RN, BSN

ISBN 978-1-888685-51-0 (eBook) 1. Child rearing–Religious aspects–Christianity
ISBN 978-1-888685-50-3 (paperback book) 1. Child rearing–Religious aspects–Christianity

Turansky, Scott, 1957-
Miller, Joanne, 1960-

Title. The Family Challenge
Passing the Faith from Your Heart to Theirs

You may obtain a free eBook of this book by going to www.biblicalparenting.org/thefamilychallenge.asp

The names of people who have come to the National Center for Biblical Parenting for counseling have been changed. Some illustrations combine individual stories in order to protect confidentiality. Stories of the authors' children have been used by permission.

The National Center for Biblical Parenting is a nonprofit corporation committed to the communication of sound, biblical parenting principles through teaching, counseling, and publishing written, audio, and video materials.

To obtain a complete resource list or have Dr. Scott Turansky and Joanne Miller present their material live, you may contact the National Center for Biblical Parenting, 76 Hopatcong Drive, Lawrenceville, NJ 08648-4136, (800) 771-8334 or visit the website at: www.biblicalparenting.org

You may also want to take online parenting courses at Biblical Parenting University. Learn more at www.biblicalparentinguniversity.com

Also, if you haven't done so already, would you please commit to taking the Family Challenge at www.414familychallenge.com and see the numbers increase in your area of the world.

You may email us at parent@biblicalparenting.org

Table of Contents

Why does this book start with chapter 2?
See the first page of this book.

2

God Designed the Plan

If parents have an unnoticeable faith, that's the faith they're passing on to their kids.

The Family Challenge

I t's surprising how similar the believers in Moses' day, who were getting ready to enter the Promised Land, are to us in the twenty-first century. Let's look at the story.

In the book of Deuteronomy, the believers are preparing to possess the Land of Canaan. Over the last several years, they've learned to trust the Lord in their own lives as they wandered in the wilderness. Now, they want to move forward to obey God and serve him. The book of Deuteronomy is the story of the rededication of their lives and the instructions given by God of how to go forward with him, both personally and in their families.

These believers were headed into a new land where a number of evil influences threatened their spiritual health. Huge temptations loomed for their children. The people who currently lived in the land had practices that went against God's values. How would they be successful in a world that was so pagan? These people were just like us. They loved God, loved their kids, wanted to serve the Lord, and they wanted to raise families committed to him. They would need to do that, living in a land that had evil influences and temptations that could rob them of the blessings of God.

It's interesting to note that in the past forty years all of the men of fighting age had died in the wilderness. That was part of God's judgment on the people for being unwilling to obey his leadership. It means, then, that likely there were a number of single parents and blended families among the Israelite nation. The instructions given to the people by Moses apply to every form of family out there, not just to traditional families. The instructions are for moms, dads, grandparents, adoptive parents, and anyone caring for kids.

As the Old Testament story unfolds, the people will go forward and do great things for God. But many would also fail. Some children would marry pagan wives. Sin was waiting at every turn. What would make these believers successful, living in a world full of pitfalls on all sides? The answer is found in Moses' instructions to them in Deuteronomy chapter 6. He starts by telling the parents what they must do. Verse 6 says, "These commandments that I give you today are to be upon your hearts."

Discipleship in the family starts with the commitment of parents to the commands of God. Raising children is the most challenging experience you'll probably ever have. Your commitment to the Lord will help you get through the tough times and know how to help your child through many challenges of life. The Bible contains the wisdom that you'll need to teach your kids how to deal with sibling conflict, how to accept no as an answer, and how to respond well to correction. God provides tools and methodology, and the more you study God's Word, the easier it will be for your children to receive the faith that has empowered you.

The passage continues in verses 7-9 by giving specific instructions for parents. "Impress them on your children. Talk about them when you sit at home and when you walk along the road, when you lie down and when you get up. Tie them as symbols on your hands and bind them on your foreheads. Write them on the doorframes of your houses and on your gates."

You can break down those instructions into three principles: Build Relationship, Share Scripture, and Practice Faith. Those three principles form the basis of the "how to" presented in this book.

You *Build Relationship* by being with your kids when they sit at home, are traveling in the van, at bedtimes, and morning times. Building relationship provides the vehicle through which values pass from one generation to the next. But building relationship with your kids is not enough.

You also need to *Share Scripture*. God says in the passage that parents are to impress the commands of God on their children. Sharing scripture with kids helps them see that the Bible is relevant, practical, and exciting. The commands of God are the standard by which we live. We are all accountable to God for our lives.

Practicing Faith actually shows children how to apply the Scriptures to their lives. They learn in practical ways what it means to demonstrate faith, hope, and love. Actions such as prayer, Bible study, service, compassion, money management, and commitment to God's church come out of the commands of God. Children pick up their faith from their parents, whatever that faith is.

Kids learn from their parents how to handle unfairness, manage resources, and think about others. If you're connected to God and his Word, then kids will see what it means to serve God in practical ways. Children are learning a biblical worldview as they live in a home where parents are seeking to serve the Lord. No greater gift can equip your children to be successful.

Later in Deuteronomy 6:20-24, Moses further explains how parents can Build Relationship, Share Scripture, and Practice Faith. He instructs them to tell stories about their own faith and that of others. He says, "In the future, when your son asks you, 'What is the meaning of the stipulations, decrees and laws the Lord our God has commanded you?' tell him: 'We were slaves of Pharaoh in Egypt, but the Lord brought us out of Egypt with a mighty hand. Before our eyes the Lord sent miraculous signs and wonders—great and terrible—upon Egypt and Pharaoh and his whole household. But he brought us out from there to bring us in and give us the land that he promised on oath to our forefathers. The Lord commanded us to obey all these decrees and to fear the Lord our God, so that we might always prosper and be kept alive, as is the case today.' "

Children benefit from hearing faith stories from your life and from the lives of others. It helps them put their own faith into the context of history. As you tell children how you committed your life to Christ and stories about how you made subsequent decisions to follow him, they see that godliness is personal. Kids benefit from listening to you tell how God has provided for you, answered your prayers, and shown care for you personally as well as to your family. As you have opportunity, allow your children to hear the stories of your friends and others who have made commitments to Jesus Christ.

One dad took his fourteen-year-old son to hear a baseball player share his faith story at a men's event at church. The boy was struck with the fact that this man was working out his faith as a sports figure. The experience led to some helpful dialogue between this father and his son. Our world is rich with stories of people who are demonstrating that their faith is more than just a church experience. Faith forms the basis for their lives. Children can learn that now. They don't have to wait until they're grownups to become Christians. They can serve God now in every area of their lives.

Each child has a story too. As you have opportunity, ask your child questions about personal faith. Be on the lookout for opportunities for your kids to share what God is teaching them. An answer to prayer or a Bible lesson learned, gives children a testimony of God's grace in their own lives.

Pierre was fifteen years old when he was arrested with some other boys his age for throwing rocks at cars on the road. His parents were shocked. They had raised him to know better. They were a Christian family and couldn't believe that their son was involved with other kids to do something so foolish and dangerous. The event led to some significant dialogue, a change in friends, and tighter limits on their son. A few weeks later, they accompanied their son to court, but allowed Pierre to face the judge and the consequence of community service for his offense.

But here's an interesting thing that happened to this family. Mom and Dad had just heard a sermon about the importance of being intentional about passing the faith on to children. God used the teaching at church to help them realize that they hadn't worked on it enough in their home. Sure, they took their son to church for years and had him attend youth group, but at home, there wasn't much talk about spiritual things. Dad and Mom decided to make a change by

13

sharing their faith more spontaneously and openly and by having at least one Family Time per week centered on the Bible.

At first, Pierre was resistant, viewing the Family Time as part of his punishment, but that quickly changed. Mom made the time special with a favorite dessert, and Dad looked for ways to communicate biblical truth through activity and fun. On one occasion they talked about Jesus' warning to the disciples in Luke 12:1, "Be on your guard against the yeast of the Pharisees, which is hypocrisy." They did an experiment with yeast by putting a packet of yeast mixed with water into a six-inch Ziploc bag with a tablespoon of sugar. Within an hour, the bag had expanded with carbon dioxide.

Pierre thought the experiment was interesting, and it provided an opportunity for he and his parents to talk about Jesus' warning to his disciples. Jesus wanted them to be on guard about the influence of the Pharisees on their lives. Dad explained that, in the same way that yeast changes the physical constitution of the solution in the plastic bag, bad influences in our lives change the constitution of our character.

Change began to take place in Pierre's life over the next several weeks. Mom described it this way: "Pierre is changing. He seems to be more careful about his friends and is making choices that aren't as self-focused as we've seen in the past. He's thinking about others and seems to be more sensitive to what God is doing around us. I'm sure that going to court and our firmer discipline has helped, but I would say that the increased spiritual activity in our family has also contributed greatly."

When asked about how things were different now in his life than they had been two months prior, Pierre said, "I realized that what I did was stupid. I shouldn't have done what the other guys were doing. I just got caught up in the moment." When asked how his family is helping him to grow and to be strong, he made an interesting statement: "I have a great family. My dad and mom are Christians and they're teaching me how to live like a Christian too."

Pierre has a lot to learn, and so do his parents, but the reality is that they're all growing in their faith as a family. Dad and Mom are being more transparent about their spiritual lives and regularly look for creative ways to pass the faith on to their son. They pray together as a family and talk about what they're learning in their lives. Their willingness to be vulnerable and help their son understand biblical truths is influencing Pierre significantly. It's not always easy, but they're determined to help their son understand what faith in God looks like in practical terms.

As the Deuteronomy believers faced the challenge of conquering the Promised Land, they and their children encountered a number of obstacles. One of those was living in an environment that had ungodly influences all around. Deuteronomy 7 describes the nations that presently lived in that land. Their ungodliness created temptations that would be hard to withstand. God wanted his people to be successful in the midst of all of the challenges they would face. That's why he gave the instructions in Deuteronomy 6:6-9 mentioned above. It's the same today. When parents are active in their faith, transparent in their spiritual growth, and eagerly passing on the faith to their kids, then those children are better equipped to face the challenges all around them.

Your kids are bombarded with worldly influences. How will they think about living their lives as chosen people entering a Promised Land full of blessings? Sticking true to God and his instructions will protect them from the myriad of temptations and pitfalls. It's great to provide your kids with spiritual activities and a good church where they can learn and grow, but nothing can replace the impact of your role as spiritual discipler of your children. It's powerful. It's God's design.

Our goal in this section of the book is to lay out for you a practical plan to pass the faith on to your kids. We call it the Family Challenge. When you take the Family Challenge and commit to Build Relationship, Share Scripture, and Practice Faith with at least one structured time each week, great things will happen in you and your kids. And your family itself will grow closer together. The next few chapters will show you how to make it happen in your family in practical ways.

4

Relationship is Foundational

FAMILY is the most influential human relationship in people's lives, whether they want it to be or not!

The Family Challenge

As you seek to pass the faith on to your children, you'll want to combine the three strategies from Deuteronomy 6: Build Relationship, Share Scripture, and Practice Faith. In this chapter, we'll discuss the first strategy of building relationship, since that's the channel through which the other two components become effective. Building relationship is foundational for passing the faith on to your kids.

So what is relationship and how do you build it? Relationship is more than just living together as a family. Relationship implies a deeper connection. It's a heart response toward one another that says, "I know you, I like you, I enjoy being with you." When parents and children have a strong relationship, they value one another and are open to learn.

Building relationship comes naturally for some parents but is more difficult for others. Nonetheless, it's not optional. Close relationships between parents and children are the tool to help kids catch the convictions they'll need to be the world changers God intends.

So how do you do it? Relationships don't just happen, and certainly maintaining close relationships takes work. Some parents find connecting with young children easy. They curl up on the couch for a special read-aloud or a favorite movie. The shared experience leads to gentle hugs and feelings of closeness. Tickling games, fun desserts, cute nicknames, and family outings all bring closeness to families with young children.

Older children connect in different ways. Conversations about feelings and opinions, playing games together, and sharing in a hobby or skill, help parents and teens to connect in heartfelt ways. Here are a few things to keep in mind when seeking to build relationship.

1. Be intentional. If you're expecting relationship to grow on its own, you may be disappointed. Take initiative to get to know your child's heart. Try different things and make mental notes about what works and what doesn't.

2. Stay focused. If the goal of an activity is to deepen closeness, then save the instruction giving and correction session for another time. Non-critical listening breeds closeness. Eye contact and physical touch say, "I'm interested in you." Parents should always be sensitive to the relational component of their parenting, but some events and activities can have the primary goal of developing closeness. In that case, you may choose to postpone interaction that may work against your goal. For the moment, you may have to look past the wiggles of a preschooler or the misplaced values of a preteen. You'll likely come back to some issues later, but in that particular activity, stay focused on relationship as much as you can. Of

course, that's not always possible. Sometimes parenting requires that you give up what you thought might be a special relational time because a child needs some form of discipline at the moment. Hopefully, though, there are times when you're able to focus on building relationship as the goal.

3. Be available. Relationships don't always grow on a schedule. Your elementary age child may open her heart to you just as you're trying to tuck her in at night. Your teenager may come home from an activity and be eager to talk. Be on the lookout for opportunities when your child is reaching out to you. It may be subtle or at a "bad" time, but, if possible, stop what you're doing and give your full attention.

4. Activities help. Working together to accomplish a goal is a great relationship-building tool. Cleaning the garage, making a new recipe for dinner, or going on a family trip to the park all have the potential to deepen relationship. Working and playing together build connection.

5. Develop traditions. Family traditions bring closeness and develop strong family bonds. Holiday traditions, vacation traditions, or even Saturday morning breakfast traditions all contribute to relationship building.

6. Watch your timing and listen. Sometimes older children respond well to being treated like adults.

Sometimes they need to relive tender moments in more playful ways. Building relationship requires careful observation and sensitivity in order to meet kids where they're at and connect in ways that touch their hearts.

Remember, however, that building relationship is not an end in and of itself. Some parents miss this truth and end up with a family that's self-focused. God has given the family a bigger purpose to embrace. A strong family is one that seeks to bless others, cares for people, and is a place where people can find God in tangible ways.

In short, the family is a place where children become disciples of Jesus Christ. Next, they learn how to become disciple-makers themselves. Some parents miss these essential goals, believing instead that they are simply trying to raise mature, responsible kids. Yet God designed the family to be a disciple-making center, where children learn what it means to serve the Lord and then reach out and help others see what a life committed to God is all about. That family can be a strategic vehicle for transforming the world. Children learn how to hold convictions, solve problems, and communicate a biblical worldview in a way that advances God's kingdom in the home, neighborhood, school, and the world.

Biblical principles are taught in the home in everyday experiences such as handling conflict, working on chores, and getting ready in the morning. Close relationships between parents and children are important because they mimic the kind of love that God has for his children. Relationship is foundational and God uses his relationship with us to help us learn and grow. In the same way, your relationship with your children is a springboard for helping them catch the convictions they'll need to be the world changers God intends.

Relationship is more than just spending time together. Relationship involves connecting with a child's heart. Some parents think that when the family jobs are complete, then they can enjoy some much-needed rest, but typically additional times of relationship building are necessary to develop strong family bonds. One very committed mom who homeschooled her kids said, "I used to think that I was earning all the relationship points I needed by homeschooling my kids each day, but then I realized that my children needed more from me. I needed to spend time with them enjoying relationship outside of school time in order to experience closeness with my kids."

The essence of parenting is relationship, not parental business. Before parents enter into the business of parenting, they're in relationship with their children. Relationship comes before duty. It's true that parents must engage in the business of parenting by giving instructions, correcting, and setting limits. Those are very important parts of a parent's job description. Keep in mind, though, that those things often put pressure on the relationship. Therefore, it's important to intentionally work on building relationship with each of your children. Since being a parent can quickly focus on tasks, it's important that parents seek ways to connect emotionally even among the jobs of family life. It's when the relational connectedness between family members decreases significantly that tension increases, and a parent's ability to teach and influence decreases as well.

Two parenting strategies help increase the closeness among family members. Both take time, and they each approach the challenge in different ways. The first is initiative, and the second is responsiveness. Both require margin or extra time in the schedule and flexibility in one's personal agenda.

Initiative looks for ways to consider the other person's interests, needs, and desires. What is your child's favorite food, color, friend, or activity? What are the top three stressors in your teen's life? What longings, hopes, and desires does your child have? When you know the answers to these kinds of questions, then you can initiate in meaningful ways. Children see that you care when you take interest in the details and passions of their lives. It might be by making their favorite cookies or bringing home an idea from work that delights your child. You see your daughter's eyes light up and you know that you've touched her heart. You might ask yourself, "What can I do to bring joy into my child's life?" It's not about giving things to a child; it's about knowing your child's heart and demonstrating that you care.

Because each child is unique and different, it's easier to connect with some kids than it is with others. Some children are external processors so you know everything they're thinking, providing easy opportunities to identify interests in common and areas to pursue. Internal processors may be more of a puzzle to their parents and might need different ways to experience closeness with Mom or Dad. Likewise, some kids are loud and demanding; others are naturally more sensitive and compassionate.

Remember that the daily work of family life typically results in a slow drain on relationship. Getting the house cleaned up, kids ready in the morning, homework done, and taxiing kids from one location to another can be a challenge for any manager. The work involved to get food on the table and clothes cleaned is stressful and has the potential to put pressure on family relationships. Initiating relationship regularly is like adding oil to the machine to reduce friction in order to make the tasks easier to accomplish.

Initiative is proactive. Responsiveness, on the other hand, puts you in observation mode, always on the lookout for an opportunity to connect. Responsiveness keeps a ready attitude for those moments when your child expresses a need, an exciting moment, or a desire to talk. The child who is overwhelmed with excitement about a new opportunity, or discouraged by a disappointing event, both have one thing in common—an opportunity for a parent to connect on a heart level. Although advice and problem-solving may help in those moments, it's most important to share the emotion and empathize with your child's feelings. When you do, you can connect with your child's heart.

Initiative reminds you to think about your child. Responsiveness keeps you ready for the surprises that may come along at any time. Both help contribute to relationship building, and if you take advantage of the opportunities, you may have some significant relational connections.

Opportunities for closeness regularly present themselves, but recognizing them is only part of the challenge. The other part is bringing faith into life in practical ways. That doesn't mean that every emotional experience needs a Bible verse or a prayer time. That would seem artificial, especially as your children get older. But spiritual sensitivity often increases when emotions are involved. Parents can help frame the picture for their children by moving excitement to gratefulness for God's provision or

26

discouragement to relying on God's grace. Spirituality, in part, is a way of thinking, and often parents can help children integrate their faith into what might otherwise appear to be mundane everyday tasks.

Deuteronomy 6:7-9 suggests four opportunities for relationship building. When you sit at home, when you walk along the road, when you lie down, and when you get up. In reality, this passage talks about all aspects of life together, but translated into modern times, we can interpret it to mean when you're hanging out at home, going somewhere, in the morning, and at bedtimes. Those are four strategic times that provide relationship opportunities.

One mom affirmed the benefit of traveling together by saying, "When we're in the van I have a captive audience. I try to plan stimulating questions or stories to get kids talking and interacting. We require some of our van time to be without electronics. Video games are shut down, headphones get put away, and the radio is off. It usually takes a bit of recovery time for kids to reenter a relational mode. They don't often bounce right into conversation having been fully engaged in an electronic battle with the universe. In fact, sometimes they even resent having to leave their electronic friends. I know that it takes a bit of time to disengage with electronics and start connecting relationally, so I'm patient to allow that to happen. Typically after a few minutes, a lively conversation erupts. Sometimes we share about our day, and other times we talk about something that's happening, or share opinions about an idea."

Storytelling about your day, or reminiscing about past common experiences, is a good way to draw children into the conversation. When you make these practices common, children learn to create their own conversation, tell their own stories, and ask their own questions. Listening and responding to your children increases openness.

One parent shared this observation: "I longed for my daughter to learn how to drive. She's seventeen now and she's been driving for six months. I didn't realize what I'd lose when she got her driver's license. We used to talk in the car as I drove her to sports, church, and other activities. Now, she's gone a lot, driving herself to work and all of her activities. I miss our times in the car together. We're having to find new ways to connect. If I knew a year ago what I know now, I probably would have valued those together times more."

Some parents are fast enough on their feet to pass the faith on to their kids spontaneously. But most parents realize an opportunity after the fact, or see one developing but don't quite know how to respond in the moment. After a little while, in that case, a parent may return to a child and say, "I like what you shared during dinner today. I just want you to know that I'm praying for you." Or, "Yesterday you were talking about that problem you're having at school and I found a verse that might be helpful for you."

The impact of Sharing Scripture and Practicing Faith is much greater when it takes place in the context of Building Relationship. That's why we're encouraging you to take the Family Challenge. Passing the faith on to kids takes place spontaneously throughout the day, but often requires a planned time for more structured teaching.

The Build Relationship part of the Family Challenge makes your times more meaningful, and the heart connection gives opportunity for children to connect with God. It may be a favorite meal shared or laughing together over a book of riddles. It could be an activity that engages everyone in the family, or just a simple conversation that sets the stage for the time together. As you look for ways to build relationship you're teaching children an important value in life: relationships are important. In fact, parents can become facilitators to help children connect with God himself. And of course that's the goal. You have a significant role as a parent. Passing on the faith doesn't only happen by reading God's Word at the table after dinner. It takes place in the daily interactions of life through the relationships you have with your kids.

5

Scripture + Creativity = Impact

Read God's Word and it will grow in your heart.
Read God's Word with your kids
and it will grow in theirs.

The Family Challenge

W hen Jesus wanted to communicate a kingdom principle, he combined it with a story
of a man walking on the road or a seed growing in the
ground. We call that teaching strategy "parables." The
creativity helped imbed the truth into the hearts of
the hearers. In the same way that Jesus used stories,
parents can use the language of children, which is
activity, to communicate God's truth. Kids of any age
learn through play, and what better way to help them
understand the principles of scripture than through
activity.

"But I don't have a creative bone in my body,"
said one interested mom. That may seem true, but
most people are more creative than they think, and
there are many resources and tools that help parents
use activity to teach children about the Bible. You'll
be surprised with the creative ideas you can come up
with yourself when you're studying the scriptures and
then talking to your child about them. The goal is to
help kids recognize that the Bible is relevant, practical, and exciting.

When you read the Bible to your children, you
want them to know that it's different than any other
book. At the end of the story, take a moment and ask
the question, "What's the lesson learned?" We don't
just read the Bible for entertainment, although it's
captivating. Rather, the Bible is God's message to us,
and one never knows what will happen when the

scripture is heard or read. Hebrews 4:12 says, "For the word of God is living and active. Sharper than any double-edged sword, it penetrates even to dividing soul and spirit, joints and marrow; it judges the thoughts and attitudes of the heart."

Before you open the Bible, you might say with anticipation in your voice, "Son, I'm about to open the Bible. Are you ready? It's alive and I'm not sure what will happen when I open it. But I know that this book is powerful. It changes our hearts. Today might be the day that God convicts me to apologize to someone for something I said that was hurtful. Or, God might speak to me in the next few minutes about something important he wants me to do. Today, God might reveal a new aspect about his love for me. I don't know what he's going to say to you or to me, but I'm about to open up God's Word to find out."

Reading the Bible is a time of excitement and anticipation. Sometimes God simply confirms his love, or reminds us of his character and grace. Other times he prompts us to action or places a burden on our hearts to think differently or change a way that we live. You never know what might happen when you open God's Word.

The word "devotions" in some families means sitting around a table and reading a passage of scripture. Although some children may find that approach helpful, it's very adult-like, and often doesn't take into account the fact that God made kids to wiggle and be silly. Why not use silliness to your advantage and movement to teach God's Word? Teens benefit from logical discussions involving biblical passages, but they also appreciate it when the lesson is illustrated in practical ways. As much as it may seem that your teens don't want to be with you, teens really do want to know what their parents think, and they want their parents to know what they think too.

In one family Dad determined to create a commentary on the book of Proverbs with his teenage sons. They would read a chapter and then ask the question, "What verse in that chapter might we add to our pages?" They would identify a particular verse about something such as listening, money, or anger, and then Dad would say, "What's the lesson we learn from that verse?" Then, spread out on the dining room table, they had about 25 different pieces of paper, each one with a title at the top, representing a subject referred to in the book of Proverbs. There were pages dedicated to anger, friends, money, wisdom, speech, and many more topics. One of the page headings was "the immoral woman" and whenever the book of Proverbs had something to say about that subject, the boys took notice and they wrote down the lessons learned. They were very interested in that subject and the conversations about sex made a lasting impact.

That commentary was never published, although

it would have been a special book. Maybe it would have been called, "A Commentary on the Book of Proverbs by a Dad and His Sons." But it was published in the hearts of those boys. They learned to love God's Word and to value the book of Proverbs and the wisdom that it provides.

When you regularly pull out the Bible in family life, you teach children a very important lesson, that the scriptures are our authority for life. The Bible is our standard and has answers for addressing the challenges we face every day.

Over the past several years there's been an explosion in the number of children's Bibles. These Bibles have pictures, illustrations, and age-appropriate communication styles. They engage children with the scriptures, helping them realize that the Bible is relevant for them now. It's exciting and practical for their daily living. The reason you want to purchase age-appropriate Bibles for your children is to communicate that the scriptures are for them now, and they apply to their lives. It's not just a book that they'll find interesting when they get to be adults.

One grandpa told this story. "I bought an early reader Bible for my six-year-old grandson. He immediately opened it up to the story of Moses and the burning bush and started to read the words on the page. He couldn't read them all, so I helped him, but it was clearly a text designed for children who were just learning how to read. My grandson loved the fact that he could read the Bible. He held that book tightly in his arms and proclaimed, 'This is my Bible.' "

One of the goals parents have is to change some of the erroneous beliefs kids have in their hearts. For example, some kids believe that "When my brother is annoying, I have the right to punch him." Or, "If I'm unhappy with life situations, I can display my displeasure with whining, complaining, or a bad attitude." Or, "My job description in life is to have fun and anything that looks like work should be avoided at all cost." These beliefs create tension in the relationships in family life and kids need to make some changes. It's amazing how many areas of a child's thinking can be corrected by looking at God's Word. The study of the Bible is practical and kids learn valuable lessons about daily life when parents share the scriptures with them.

In the Jackson family, Dad and Mom were disheartened by the competition and comparison between their sons, Jamal, age eight, and Desmond, age nine. They often raced to sit in the best seat in the van or wanted the first turn at the computer. Dad and Mom decided to read them the story of the two guys in the Bible who wanted the best seat. Mark 10 tells the story. James and John came to Jesus and said, "Let one of us sit at your right and the other at your left in your glory" (v. 37). Jesus' answer to them was, "Whoever wants to become great among you must be your servant, and whoever wants to be first must be slave of all."

Dad and Mom then created the "Upside Down Game" to illustrate this biblical truth in a playful way. They had a race to see who could serve others the most in a five-minute period and they kept track with points on a piece of paper. Dad said to Mom, "I just want to tell you how pretty you are." Dad got a point. Mom got up and started to rub Dad's shoulders. She got a point. The boys started to join in, first to Dad and Mom and then with each other. Jamal said, "Desmond, you're really good at baseball." Jamal got a point. The game was enjoyable and when the time was up, they talked about the value of service and putting others first. Not only was it a fun family experience, but it also generated a different way of thinking for the boys over the next few days. Dad and Mom were able to talk about having an attitude of servanthood instead of wanting to be first or best.

The goal is to pass the faith on to kids so that they'll put biblical truths into practice. But how is faith developed in the life of a child? God gives the answer in Romans 10:17, "Faith comes from hearing the message, and the message is heard through the word of Christ." As parents open the Bible regularly with their children and talk about the lessons learned from God's Word, then a child's faith begins to grow. It's nurtured through more Bible stories and applications that apply to them. A constant diet of the scriptures provides children with a way to think about themselves, about God, and about their purpose in life.

If you go to the doctor, he might give you a prescription and tell you, "Take this pill once a day and come back and see me in a week." A similar thing can happen in our spiritual lives by immersing ourselves in God's Word on a regular basis. The Bible isn't a quick fix. It provides deep, long-lasting solutions for life. If, for example, you're having troubles and challenges, you might read about heaven in Revelation 21-22 every day for a week and see what impact it has on your heart. Meditating on heaven can help us get our minds on spiritual things and give us some perspective on life's challenges.

If your child has a problem with selfishness, then it would certainly be helpful to do some teaching about the biblical concept of honor. It's important to be careful about over-using God's Word in correction so that a child doesn't develop a punitive picture of God. Often presenting the solutions from God's Word in a positive way gives children a vision for something better. It may be that memorizing Romans 12:10, "Honor one another above yourselves," or Philippians 2:3-4, "Do nothing out of selfish ambition or vain conceit, but in humility consider others better than yourselves. Each of you should look not only to your own interests, but also to the interests of others," may be just the therapy that helps bring about a positive change in your child.

God's Word is relevant and every area of family life provides opportunity for its application. The Bible contains the secret ingredients children need to be successful in life, both now and for their futures. That's why it's so important for parents to spend time learning God's Word themselves and then passing the truths on to their children. Using fun, activity, and play help kids receive the truths.

The Family Challenge encourages spontaneous integration of the Bible with life, but by taking the challenge, you also agree to plan at least one structured time per week. A planned Family Time of 20-30 minutes of fun devotions can open the door for many spontaneous opportunities to apply that same truth for weeks to come.

Consider taking the Family Challenge. Schedule a regular time once a week to intentionally pass the faith on to your kids. As you Build Relationship, Share Scripture, and Practice Faith, you'll see the difference in your family. Your kids will begin to think and act differently. It's encouraging to watch children grow in God's grace. At the heart of spiritual growth is an understanding of God's Word. Your commitment to God and his Word in your family will have a marked effect on you and your kids for the rest of their lives.

6

Practicing Faith Teaches that it's Real

If grasping faith for kids is like learning to drive, then the church is the classroom and the home is behind the wheel.

F aith is practical. It results in action. Faith forms the basis for our lives, both as children and as adults. Faith isn't just Bible lessons learned at church. Faith isn't just encouragement that helps us get through the day. Faith is the foundation we build our lives upon. It affects everything we do. It's more than just mental assent or head knowledge. Faith is our life.

James 2:14 asks the question, "What good is it, my brothers, if a man claims to have faith but has no deeds?" Then he answers it a few verses later in 2:26, "As the body without the spirit is dead, so faith without deeds is dead." It's important to put our faith to the test by applying it regularly to our lives. Faith works itself out in who we are.

Faith must be practical for kids to grab hold of it. Parents pass the faith on to their children by practicing it with them. The Christian life is more than words and teaching; it's action. When parents put faith into practice, it begins to live in their hearts. When parents practice faith with their children, it begins to live in the hearts of their children as well.

When you take time to pray with your kids about life situations, then they get to see the power of God at work. You don't have to be afraid that your kids will get discouraged just because God doesn't give them exactly what they want when they pray for it.

Through prayer children learn that God isn't a genie. He's God. He wasn't created for our benefit to make us happy. We were created for him and we seek to discover his will.

Practicing faith is done in many ways and takes on many faces. Ask yourself how you practice faith, and then invite your kids to participate with you. When a dad announces that he's learning to be more compassionate and looks for ways to show it to others, kids take notice. They see God actually working in Dad's heart. When a mom asks forgiveness for yelling at her son, he sees God active in his mom's heart. True faith in any of our lives changes how we live. It affects our actions and the way we think about life. Kids benefit from seeing that kind of faith in action.

Spiritual transparency can take place in the normal conversations of life. It may have been that in the past that you saw a beautiful sunset, felt gratefulness to God, and shot up a prayer of admiration for his creativity and beauty. But it was done in private. Now, you say it out loud, "God, that sure is a beautiful sunset you made." You're not trying to concoct something that isn't there. You're just revealing your spirituality to your children.

If you go back to Deuteronomy 6:20-21, you see one of the practical ways to practice faith with your kids: answer their questions using faith and your spiritual history. "In the future, when your son asks you, 'What is the meaning of the stipulations, decrees and laws the Lord our God has commanded you?' tell him." The passage goes on to give spiritual history. Children often ask the question, "Why?" "Why do I have to do this?" "Why are you saying no?" Just as it's okay for us to ask respectful questions of God, it's good for our children to learn to ask respectful questions of us.

When children ask questions, it's often a good time to share convictions, beliefs, and the legacy of your spiritual faith. Even if you've recently come to Christ, you can share about how important he is to you now and how you desire to serve him with all your heart.

Your family rules come from your convictions, and many of those convictions come straight from the Bible. Even those that don't are often examples of your desire to live out your faith. If you tell your son to come for dinner, and he, not wanting to stop his activity, says, "I'm not hungry," you now have an opportunity to teach about a conviction you have. His belief is that mealtime is simply for satisfying his appetite and if he's not hungry, then coming to the table isn't necessary. You, on the other hand, believe that mealtime is more than that. You want your family together and the social component of the meal is even more important than the food. Thus, your training in the moment provides the practical application your child needs to experience the faith. Your convictions demonstrate your value of family relationships.

You have reasons behind your rules, and each rule is a demonstration of your convictions. You clean up the house because of a sense of stewardship. Your family doesn't allow siblings to hit each other to solve problems, because you want to teach kindness and more constructive forms of problem solving. You use manners to show honor to others, and try to get somewhere on time to demonstrate your integrity. As children live in your home, they're experiencing the rules of your family that come out of your convictions. But many times they see the rules and not what's behind them. This is a reality that's even difficult for many adults to understand. Regular discussions with your kids about the convictions behind the rules often reveal how you're living out your faith in daily life. Kids then can catch the reality of what it means to love God with all your heart, soul, mind, and strength and love your neighbor as yourself.

You might say to your daughter who is headed out the door, "I'll be praying for you today as you try to work out that problem with your friend." Or, "Son, would you please pray for me. I'm not feeling too well and I have an important meeting at work." Those kinds of prayers acknowledge the need for God, but they also demonstrate that you're living every day in a way that relies on God's grace. You believe that he has answers and that he cares about you in the personal, daily needs of life.

When Jesus was teaching his disciples to pray he included these words, "Give us this day our daily bread." That phrase implies the need to come to God regularly for his provision and care. Prayer not only changes others, but it changes us. When we pray for a grumpy neighbor, we often find ourselves more sensitive to his needs and patient when relating to him. As kids pray for help for a problem with a friend and ask for strength to get through a difficult project, they see God answer their prayers. This further strengthens their faith.

Some parents feel uncomfortable praying out loud. They often view prayer as a private activity and their faith as very personal. Those things are true, but praying with others, especially children, is a great way to allow kids to experience the grace of God themselves. One mom said, "I realized that I was limiting our family's spiritual growth because of my fear of praying out loud. I determined to get over it, and praying with my kids proved to be the training ground I needed. I was so touched by the simple, real prayers of my children, that I was able to pray out loud with them. Now I feel much more comfortable praying in a group of adults when the opportunity arises. I realized that it's not about having the right words. It's about connecting my heart to God."

Some parents develop good habits of praying before meals or before bed. Those are great exercises of faith, but be careful that you have other times when you talk about prayer and God's Word. You don't want your children to believe that God only shows up at mealtime and bedtime. God is ever present and eagerly seeks relationship with us.

One dad had his watch beep every hour for a while. His kids asked him why he was doing that. His answer was, "I want to remind myself that my time is God's time so every time it beeps I just say a short prayer to God, thanking him for this next hour. It helps me be ready for the interruptions that often happen around here. Instead of getting frustrated with them, now I try to look at the interruptions as opportunities in one way or another."

When children watch their parents trying to live out their faith, good things happen. That doesn't mean that we have to be perfect. Kids can learn from our imperfections as well. Saying "I'm sorry" to a child demonstrates humility. Admitting that you're working on something in your life, such as keeping calm under pressure, is helpful for kids to see. The family is a laboratory for growth for parents and for their kids. Offering and receiving grace is a demonstration of faith and helps children integrate their spiritual lives into the rest of who they are.

Another way that parents can communicate the faith is by serving others outside the family. Giving money, time, or energy can help kids learn to think about others and not just their own needs. In one family, the parents responded to a desire their son had to serve. This young boy heard about disease and suffering in Africa and wanted to help provide clean drinking water for the people there. The family asked for permission to set up a table at their church and raised money to give to an organization that built wells in villages that didn't have clean water.

Looking for opportunities to work together to serve others is a practical way to demonstrate faith. Serving in a soup kitchen, visiting a nursing home, sending gifts to a missionary, or shoveling snow off a neighbor's sidewalk are all ways to live out your faith with your children.

Sometimes the family can become rather self-focused with so many activities complicating the schedule. Although kids benefit from activity and events, sometimes they develop the impression that life is all about them, their needs, their development, and their accomplishments. It's good to give to others, and the earlier children learn that the better. When we give money, time, and talents, we give a bit of our own selfishness away in the process. It's part of God's design for giving.

As you plan your family's time, be careful that

you don't allow it to plan you. When you take the Family Challenge you set aside a particular period of time for the Lord as a family. It may be only 20-30 minutes a week, but that strategic time can produce a powerful impact on the lives of your children. In addition, you'll learn to live your faith out spontaneously in visible, practical ways. Thus, you'll be intentional about passing the faith on to kids through Building Relationship, Sharing Scripture, and Practicing Faith.

14

Will You Take the Family Challenge?

*Send your son to church — spiritually feed
him for a day.
Live it out at home — spiritually feed
him for life.*

The Family Challenge

Now we come to the place in the book where we ask you to make a commitment. We've discussed the importance of passing on the faith, given you tools, and provided helpful strategies to make it happen. But simply reading about it doesn't impact the family. It's the action that has a lasting influence. Will you take the Family Challenge?

Taking the Family Challenge simply means being intentional about passing the faith on to your kids both spontaneously as opportunities arise and through at least one structured Family Time each week. The Family Challenge contains three ingredients: Build Relationship, Share Scripture, and Practice Faith. As you determine to do these three things, your kids will see more clearly what it means to follow God and serve him wholeheartedly. Take a minute and pray that God would give you direction and wisdom as you take on the Family Challenge. Decide now, before you read further. What will be your next step?

Most parents have parenting books sitting on their shelves that they haven't read. Still more have books that they've read but haven't put into action. So, before you put this book aside, develop a plan for using something that you've learned in these pages. There's nothing like a plan for energizing you to action. A plan provides a goal, next steps, and generates hope to move forward in the face of challenges.

The Family Challenge

Change in a family will always meet resistance. People find themselves in patterns and even if those patterns aren't the best, people tend to stay in them because they're familiar. If you're going to make some changes, then you'll need to persevere for several weeks. Over time, you'll help your family act differently, think differently, and learn to trust God for the challenges they'll face.

Any call to commitment is a challenge to one's heart. The heart contains things like desires, commitment, emotions, passion, and convictions. Just because something comes from the heart, though, doesn't make it good. Some people's desires or emotions prompt them to put off goals, give up when facing challenges, or take on other commitments that compete with the most important things of their lives.

To help you establish your desire to move forward to intentionally pass the faith to your kids, let's look at three words that describe things in the heart according to God's Word: Conviction, Commitment, and Passion. When your heart is in it, then there's very little that can deter you from progress toward your goal. You'll need all three of these as you seek to take the Family Challenge in your home.

Conviction: The Bible teaches that convictions take place in the heart. A conviction is a belief that's so important, it results in action. You know the story of Daniel. He was certainly a man of conviction. The Bible tells us, "Daniel purposed in his heart that he would not defile himself with the portion of the king's meat" (Dan. 1:8 KJV). When Jeremiah described the New Covenant that God would establish, he wrote that it'll be different from the stone tablets of the old covenant. God said, "I will put my law in their minds and write it on their hearts" (Jeremiah 31:33). Notice, in both of these passages, how convictions develop in the heart and then result in outward actions. We know that beliefs take place in the heart because Paul describes salvation in terms of a heart commitment. Romans 10:9 says a key to salvation is when you "believe in your heart that God raised him from the dead."

Convictions are essential ingredients because they help manage emotions and desires, two other parts of the heart. If your *desire* to do something contrary to your goal is *high* and your conviction is *low*, then the result is the temptation to do other things rather than work toward your goal. When your convictions are stronger than your emotions and desires, then you can persist when you don't feel like it or when you'd rather do something else. An inner conviction prompts you to strive toward your goal and not be distracted or led astray.

In this book we've taken you to several scriptures to imbed your thinking about the Family Challenge into your convictions. That's because we know that if you develop strong convictions to take action in this area, you'll be far more successful at building a new culture in your family. If your conviction is based on Scripture, it will carry more weight in your heart.

One determined dad knew that he needed to spend time with God each day to be ready to talk to his kids. That belief prompted him to listen to three chapters of the Bible each day on his way to work. Sometimes he'd listen to more and sometimes less, but when he arrived at work, he would take two minutes in the parking lot and write down a lesson learned that would be helpful for his family. His journal became a treasure. It often just contained the scripture reference and a few lines of application, but he found himself going back to his writing over and over again in family conversations. His conviction to spend time with God made passing on the faith much easier.

Commitment: The first word is conviction. The second is commitment. Commitments start in the heart. Proverbs 3:5 says, "Trust in the Lord with all your heart." That internal desire to put God first happens deep inside a person, but it often meets other internal struggles. Commitment keeps a person on course. Commitment is a choice. In order to take the Family Challenge you'll need to be committed to the process and stick with it when resistance and distractions threaten your plans. It's amazing how one person can change a family when an underlying commitment comes from the heart.

Many obstacles will likely get in the way of your progress. Things like busyness, the attitudes of others, and resistance from a spouse are likely to slow you down at times, but your ability to hang in there after you feel like quitting is directly related to your heart. Moses knew that God's people would face many challenges when they entered the Promised Land, so he challenged them to make a commitment in their hearts to God's commands. He said, "Take to heart all the words I have solemnly declared to you this day... They are your life" (Deuteronomy 32:46-47).

Your heart is the place where it all starts. As you allow the Lord to speak to you, he will bring your heart to a place of strong commitment, so strong that you'll be able to do the work, overcome the challenges, and face the obstacles necessary for change. It won't be long before God begins to work in the hearts of other family members and your prayer is that, one by one, they too will develop a commitment to the time you spend as a family talking about God's Word.

In one family, Dad and Mom determined that they would pray together once a week. During that 20-30 minute meeting they would look at the schedule and pray for their kids. They announced to the children that they were praying for them and even asked for specific requests that they could bring before the Lord. At first, kids shared trivial things, but over time, prayer became integral in all of their lives. The commitment of these parents moved prayer to a central place in their home and resulted in a number of conversations about God's grace, power, and provision.

Passion: A third word to help you move forward is the word "passion." It's interesting to see the number of times that passion is revealed in the Bible as coming from the heart. Hezekiah was a good king who served the Lord with all his heart (2 Chronicles 31:21). David said in the psalms, "I will praise you, O Lord, with all my heart" (9:1) and "I seek you with all my heart" (119:10). In each of these verses, the word "heart" communicates the idea of passion.

When people do something wholeheartedly, they're doing it with zest and determination. Sometimes we say, "He put his heart into a job," or "She has a heart for what she's doing." Passion combines commitment, convictions, and emotion to drive the plan toward the goal.

Children see the passion of their parents when it comes to sports, money, or a hobby. Do they see that same passion about Jesus Christ? One dad, reporting about his childhood, told this story: "My mom loved Jesus. Every Saturday morning, she would gather us kids around her and she would tell us stories from the Bible. She kept us captivated as she talked about victories, tragic mistakes, and miracles in people's lives. While she talked, she'd peel apples. Each week she would peel and cut those apples and turn them into the best apple cobbler I ever tasted. Still today I have sweet memories of God's grace and power every time I smell apples and cinnamon cooking. My mother's passion for God's Word was contagious and now I enjoy reading it to my kids. I don't peel apples, but my kids know that I love Jesus just like their grandmother did."

Do you believe that God has given you the opportunity and the responsibility to pass the faith on to your kids? If you do, make it more than a belief. Turn it into a *Conviction.* Make it a *Commitment.* Allow *Passion* to fuel your goals and plans to move forward. Watch God do some amazing things in your family.

It'll be fun to see what happens to you first and then watch the little surprises that come from your kids. One little boy came to his mom and said, "Mom, I was starting to get mad and I put myself in a break to settle down. Now I'm fine." Those words were a treasure since Mom had been trying to help her son deal with anger. They had talked about the verse in James 1:19 that says, "Everyone should be quick to listen, slow to speak and slow to become angry." Mom was seeing God work in her five-year-old son. He had a long way to go but she was encouraged that God was doing a deeper work in his life already.

Many of the rewards of passing on the faith to your kids come over a period of time. You're creating a godly heritage and a faith legacy that kids will use as a foundation for years to come. The early spiritual training children receive as teens or elementary-age children, or even preschoolers, creates a vital lifeline for their own personal faith. Kids learn that God has solutions for every area of their lives. As they grow up, they'll continue to put their faith into practice. They'll see that God's Word has implications for the office, for a marriage, for friendships, and for conflict, money, and health. They'll learn to integrate their faith into life in some relevant and practical ways.

For now, though, you're building a spiritual foundation for your children. Are you committed? If so, we want to ask you to join with others around the world who are expressing their commitment to pass the faith on to their kids by taking the Family Challenge. These parents and grandparents are committing themselves to God and to their kids. They're committing to intentionally Build Relationship, Share Scripture, and Practice Faith. Take a moment and go to www.414familychallenge.com and add your commitment to hundreds of others. Then look at the map and see how God is working in the lives of parents and grandparents all over the world to pass the faith on to their kids.

The Family Challenge

If this book has blessed and challenged you, then please pass it on to someone else, or download the free eBook called Take the Family Challenge and share it with others through Facebook, at church, and through email. Or send people to our website, www. biblicalparenting.org to download it for themselves. Consider joining with us to help parents catch a vision for passing the faith on to their kids.

At the National Center for Biblical Parenting, we have a vision to empower parents to pass the faith on to their kids and to mobilize churches to equip them. We're on a mission both in the United States and around the world. We would love to have you partner with us to reach the next generation for Jesus Christ. We believe the most strategic way to make that happen is through parents. Please consider joining with us.

In the next section of this book you'll learn about moral development in children, how it happens, and how you can influence it. The study of the conscience is powerful and will help you know how to develop internal motivation in kids.

A Word to the Reader

Dear Friend,

As you know, the spiritual development of children is essential. Although many parents acknowledge this to be the case, they don't know how to pass the faith on to their kids. This book is helping people all over the world know how to live out their faith in family life. Would you consider helping us equip more parents? Maybe you'd like to give a copy of this book away to your friends or people that you meet. We want to make that easy. Please pass it on or send people to our website to download it for themselves.

We're excited about what God is doing at the National Center for Biblical Parenting. We have a very simple yet compelling vision: empowering parents to pass the faith on to their children and mobilize the church to equip them.

Maybe you've heard of the international initiative called The 4-14 Window. It's an attempt to draw young people to Christ during the most receptive period in their lives, between the ages of four and fourteen. This isn't just a work in the United States. It's international. And now, the National Center for Biblical Parenting has been chosen to be part of this global initiative. It's becoming more and more clear that God has placed us in a strategic position to make a major impact on families, both in the United States and around the globe.

The opportunity is great. We would appreciate your help. Maybe you'd consider giving a donation to help in this work. Will you join us as a financial partner? All donations are tax deductible. You can go to www.biblicalparenting.org/donate.asp to learn more.

Blessings,

Dr. Scott Turansky and Joanne Miller, RN, BSN

To make a donation, you may go to
www.biblicalparenting.org/donate.asp

**To order more copies of this book,
please call our office at (609) 771-8002**

Or you may write to us at:
The Family Challenge
National Center for Biblical Parenting
76 Hopatcong Drive
Lawrenceville, NJ 08648

A Fun Bible Activity to Do With Kids

Three Brave Friends
(Parental Supervision Required!)

Bible Story

Tell the story from Daniel 3 in your own words, highlighting the following key points:

King Nebuchadnezzar made a 90-foot-high gold idol and commanded everyone to bow down and worship the idol. If people didn't bow down then they would be thrown into a fiery furnace.

Shadrach, Meshach, and Abednego refused to bow down and worship the idol. The boys said to the king, "O Nebuchadnezzar, we do not need to defend ourselves before you in this matter. If we are thrown into the blazing furnace, the God we serve is able to save us from it, and he will rescue us from your hand, O king. But even if he does not, we want you to know, O king, that we will not serve your gods or worship the image of gold you have set up." (Daniel 3:16-18)

The king was furious and had the three boys thrown into the fiery furnace.

The soldiers who threw the boys into the furnace

were killed by the fire but Shadrach, Meshach, and Abednego were not burned or harmed.

They saw that the fire had not harmed their bodies, nor was a hair of their heads singed; their robes were not scorched, and there was no smell of fire on them. (Daniel 3:27)

Nebuchadnezzar brought the boys out of the fire and said, "Praise be to the God of Shadrach, Meshach, and Abednego." Then the boys were promoted and given more honor in Babylon.

What's the Lesson Learned?

Do the right thing, even when it's hard. That's a lesson needed by children of all ages.

Activity

Cut out three "gingerbread cookie shaped" people from a piece of corrugated cardboard. Label the three cardboard-people Shadrach, Meshach, and Abednego.

Prepare a solution that is 2 oz. rubbing alcohol (70% isopropyl) and 1 oz. water. Mix together well and put the solution on a shallow dish. Let the "people" soak in the solution. After mixing the alcohol and water move quickly to complete the activity before the alcohol evaporates.

Using paper clips, attach the three wet cardboard

people to the hanger. Hold the top of the hanger with tongs so that you can keep your body away from the fire. Remove any remaining alcohol solution and hold the hanger over a sink or safe area.

PARENTAL SUPERVISION REQUIRED. Using a lighter, light the three cardboard-people. They will be consumed in fire but will not burn. Make sure the fire is out before touching the cardboard-people. The people will not be harmed by the fire. There's no smell of smoke and they aren't even singed.

Discussion

Kids like the fire activity but remember its purpose is to teach a lesson. Ask children to repeat the lesson learned.

You might suggest some scenarios in life where kids can do the right thing, even when it's hard. If you'd like some suggestions, here are a few examples to discuss:

1 • Friends your age are watching a movie that your parents won't let you see.

The right thing to do: You choose to obey your parents.

2 • You break something important in your home.

The right thing to do: Instead of waiting for your parents to find out or denying that you were involved, you go to your parents and tell them what you did.

3 • You sit in a desk next to an unpopular girl at school.

The right thing to do: Instead of ignoring the girl, you talk with her and go out of your way to be kind.

4 • You find out your friend doesn't go to church.

The right thing to do: You invite him to go with you to your church.

Pray Together

Take a few minutes and pray that God would give strength to do the right thing this week even if it's hard.

This lesson is taken from the series, *Family Time Activities* available at biblicalparenting.org

The Family Challenge

This book is offered free through donations from people who have a passion to help parents pass the faith on to their kids.

If you're interested in more copies of this book, go to biblicalparenting.org/thefamilychallenge.asp to learn more.

If you'd like to help to get this book into the hands of others, please visit biblicalparenting.org/donate.asp.

Thank you for your partnership. We're grateful.